CRYSTAL CAVE

A GUIDEBOOK TO THE UNDERGROUND WORLD OF SEQUOIA NATIONAL PARK

BY JOEL DESPAIN

PUBLISHED BY

SEQUOIA NATURAL HISTORY ASSOCIATION

THREE RIVERS, CALIFORNIA

Cover:
Visitors to Crystal Cave walk through Marble Hall, which at one-hundred-fifty feet long and forty feet wide is the largest room in the cave. The stone formations above their heads are stalactites, one of the many types of calcite cave formations found in Crystal Cave.

Inside Cover:
A shield and stalactites hang above a rimstone pool containing water that has dripped from the tips of the stalactites. These cave formations are in the Cathedral Balconies adjacent to the Little Cathedral Room along the cave trail.

Title Page:
Visitors and their tour guide admire a large stalagmite, flowstone, stalactites and other formations in the Dome Room. This room is the second stop inside the cave in most tours.

Right:
Flowstone and cave curtains made of calcite, which in its purest form is clear. When it is white, as shown here, it contains tiny inclusions of water.

Project coordinated by **Tyler Conrad**, Executive Director, Sequoia Natural History Association
Design, typesetting, illustration, cartography and production by **Carole Thickstun** and **Larry Ormsby**
Color photography throughout the book by **Peter and Ann Bosted**, *unless noted below*
Color separations and printing by **Pioneer of Jackson Hole**, Jackson, WY

Other photo and art credits:
Flower photographs on p. 2 from National Park Service collection, Sequoia National Park
Plant illustrations on p. 4 by Jane Gyer
Ice River photo, p. 5, by Bill Frantz
(1 week after cave discovery) photo, p. 14, by Lindley Eddy
Modern cave conservation photos, p. 16, Joel Despain
Photo, p. 16, Howard Stagner
Photo, p. 17, Sam Pusateri
(early visitors to cave) photo, p. 19, by Lindley Eddy
Scallops photo, p. 28, Joel Despain
Rimstone photo, p. 34, Joel Despain
Black and white photos, p. 38-39 by Bill Frantz
Bat photos, p. 40, by Merlin Tuttle, Bat Conservation International
Lilburn Cave photos, p. 44, by Dave Bunnell
Hurricane Crawl photo, p. 45, by Dick LaForge

TABLE OF CONTENTS

Above:
A popcorn encrusted stalag-
mite in the Phosphorescent
Room on the Wild Tour
route sits behind a floor of
small rimstone dams and in
front of a wall covered by
more cave popcorn.

Right:
Rimstone in the Sugar
Cookie Passage

Below:
A complex formation con-
taining flowstone, cave pop-
corn, and cave curtains in
the Cathedral Balconies.
The sparkles in the photo
are reflections from the large
calcite crystals in the flow-
stone. This sparkling effect is
sometimes called cave velvet.

Opposite page:
A visitor to Crystal Cave in
the Dome Room. This room
contains the largest variety
of calcite cave formations in
the cave. The room is
named for the large stalag-
mite in the upper center of
the photo, which resembles
the Capitol Dome in
Washington D.C.

Right:
Stalactites hang over a floor of flowstone and stalagmites. The sparkling floor, known as cave velvet, is created when reflective crystal faces grow within the formations.

Below:
A soda straw formation in the Dome Room. This narrow, hollow variety of stalactite is very fragile and easily broken. The chemically rich water drop at the end of the soda straw is probably depositing new calcite and lengthening this formation.

Above:
A caver crawls into the Swank Room, which lies in the highest levels of Crystal Cave above Marble Hall.

INTRODUCTION

Throughout history caves have been part of people's lives. In them we have sought shelter and religious experiences. We enter their dark passages in search of adventure and explore their depths to satisfy our endless curiosity. Dark and mysterious... with winding passageways—caves serve as settings for dreams, stories, myths and legends. They represent a dark world that lies in contrast to our surface lives of sunlight and openness.

Today, scientists and explorers use modern techniques and equipment to shed new light on caves. Hydrologists study the movement of water through caves to discover how pollutants travel through groundwater. Others analyze air trapped in developing cave formations thousands of years ago for clues to climatic change.

For cave explorers—cavers—modern equipment opens up new worlds. Using reliable lights and strong, nylon ropes, cavers now chart the farthest reaches of caves—some more than a mile deep, others more than one-hundred miles long. Clinging to ropes, they descend into deep pits and cross underground rivers that roar through rapids and over waterfalls. They squeeze through narrow openings between large broken rocks. Their underground journeys may last thirty days at a time.

Crystal Cave gives visitors to Sequoia National Park an opportunity to discover the mystery and beauty of caves. In it, you can experience total darkness, and silence broken only by dripping and flowing water. Lights reveal the wonders of the cave's winding passages and many chambers. Here you can glimpse another world that's long fascinated explorers, religious worshippers, storytellers and geologists alike. Crystal Cave is protected for the experiences and information it provides, for the continuing geologic process it represents and for its value as a unique natural feature of Sequoia National Park.

A cave explorer wades through the Lake Room. This flooded room lies near the cave creek upstream from the Junction Room. The walls, ceiling and the floor of the room beneath the water are composed of large broken rocks known as breakdown.

A wide variety of flowers are along the trail to the cave. Some of the common ones are shown here.

FAREWELL TO SPRING

SCARLET MONKEYFLOWER

SPICE BUSH

HARVEST BRODEIA

INDIAN PINK

BLEEDING HEARTS

GOLDEN BRODEIA

CALIFORNIA POPPY

I

THE TRIP TO CRYSTAL CAVE

Crystal Cave lies two-thousand feet below Giant Forest at the base of a steep canyon. More than elevation separates the two. The cave has formed in an area with a different geologic history and sits within a different ecological community. The slopes near the cave mark a transition from the higher-elevation conifer forests to the oak woodlands and chaparral that dominate in the lower mountains and foothills. Plants from both communities grow here, along with other species that only grow at this elevation.

Cascade Creek flows year round, providing additional habitat for wildlife and plants. Unusual soils formed by the decomposition of marble, schist and other metamorphic rocks nurture special communities of plants and animals, further adding to the area's diversity of life.

The trail to the cave begins under a canopy of large canyon oaks. Open areas covered with mountain misery, *Ceanothus*, manzanita, poison oak and grasses offer views of the surrounding valleys and ridges. Steep, barren ridges are often composed of light-colored crystalline marble—the stone in which caves form in the Sierra Nevada. Few plants thrive in these mineralized soils derived from marble. Among the few who have adapted to them, yucca and flannel bush cling to the open ridges.

As the trail descends, other plants appear. Mock orange, California laurel and spice bush—plants common in lower-elevation wet areas—grow in the moist soil near Cascade Creek. Alongside them stand incense cedar and ponderosa pines—conifers typical of higher elevations. The trail crosses the creek below a group of small waterfalls and just above a forty-foot fall. White alders, big-leaf maples, lilies and rushes flourish in this wet environment. California nutmeg, an evergreen tree with sharp, stiff needles, and other plants unique to this elevation also grow here.

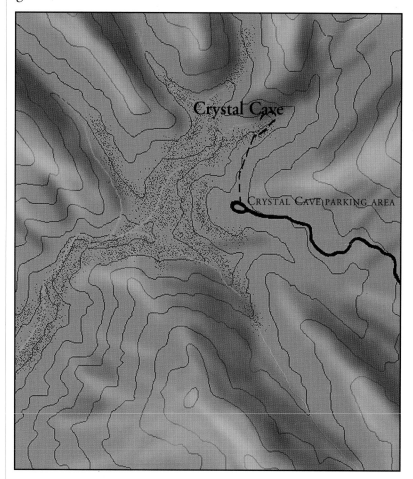

The trail to Crystal Cave drops down the hillside from the parking lot and crosses Cascade Creek. The distance is about one half mile, taking only ten or fifteen minutes to reach the cave entrance from the parking area.

3

Trees of Cascade Creek Trail

CALIFORNIA BLACK OAK

CALIFORNIA LAUREL

BIGLEAF MAPLE

LIVE OAK

INCENSE CEDAR

JEFFREY PINE

The diverse plant life near Crystal Cave supports an abundance of mammals, birds, reptiles and insects. Bear, deer and mountain lions forage along Cascade Creek. Wrens, vireos, hummingbirds and tanagers nest in the dense vegetation. Eight species of colorful and remarkably different snakes and three kinds of lizards live near the cave. Butterflies feed on the nectar of the many wildflowers that grow in the canyon. Shiny black beetles scavenge on the forest floor and, on warm summer days, throngs of ladybug beetles migrate down the valley.

The diversity of life outside Crystal Cave mirrors the beauty and variety of the mineral formations that await within its passages and rooms.

Cave Temperature & Air Flow

Air flows out of a cave with this type of passage shape and when the outside temperature is warmer than the cave.

Air flows into a large cave with this type of passage shape and when the barometric pressure outdoors is higher than the cave's internal barometric pressure.

For many visitors, the first sense of Crystal Cave comes from the cool flow of air from the Spider Web Gate entrance. Breezes of nearly twenty miles an hour have been recorded at narrow places along the entrance passage. The difference between low temperatures inside the cave and warmer summer air temperatures outside create convection currents that drive the strong air movements.

The temperature inside Crystal Cave stays a constant 48°F, which is the average outside air temperature at this elevation in the southern Sierra. The extreme temperatures of summer and winter penetrate only a few feet into rock and soil at the surface. But over thousands of years, the temperature of rock deep below the surface has adjusted to the average of summer's heat and winter's cold. Like a massive radiator set at 48° F, the solid rock of the cave walls keeps the cave air and water at the same temperature year around.

On summer days, warm air enters cracks that open into the cave from above. The air entering the cave is cooled by the 48° F rock. The cooled air sinks into the cave and draws more air down into the cracks behind it, beginning a cycle of air flow. As the air sinks down into the cave, it joins with air from other passages. The movement of air into the cave pushes the cooled air out through the Spider Web Gate entrance.

On cold winter days the process reverses. Cold air flows into the cave. As it's warmed inside the cave, it rises through the cave and flows out to the surface through cracks and passages.

Large caves with constrictions at their entrances or in passageways experience another pattern of air flow. Changes in barometric pressure at the surface, associated with passing weather fronts, create a difference in pressure between the outside air and air inside the cave. Air moves into or out of the cave: from the area of higher pressure to the one of lower pressure.

Pressure changes create cave winds of more than eighty miles an hour. This kind of air flow happens only in the largest cave systems. In the United States, winds like these sometimes roar through Carlsbad Caverns and Lechuguilla Cave in Carlsbad Caverns National Park, New Mexico and Wind Cave in Wind Cave National Park and Jewel Cave in Jewel Cave National Monument, both in South Dakota.

ICE RIVER, THREE LEVEL ICE CAVE, MEDICINE LAKE HIGHLANDS

When people think of caves, they usually have in mind something similar to Crystal Cave: formed in limestone or marble and decorated with stalactites, stalagmites and other formations. But there are several other kinds of caves.

Some caves form in lava. Flowing lava often cools unevenly. The surface and edges of a flow may harden into stone, while molten material continues to flow a few feet below the surface. Eventually the molten material drains away, leaving a hollow *lava tube.* Lava tubes vary in size and shape. Some can be as extensive and complicated as limestone and marble caves and contain many unusual features and formations. Lava tubes can be seen in Lava Beds National Monument in Northern California and also in Hawaii at Hawaii Volcanoes National Park.

Sea caves, or *littoral caves,* form along rocky coastlines where waves batter cliff faces and erode tunnels into them. Some sea caves are more than one-thousand feet long, though most are much smaller. They often feature skylights and multiple entrances. They're home to specialized marine life adapted to pounding surf and the rise and fall of tides. Some even hold wrecked ships. Unpredictable waves make sea caves dangerous places to explore. The Pacific Ocean has carved many sea caves in the edges of the Channel Islands in Channel Islands National Park off the coast of southern California.

Talus caves form where rocks cover narrow canyons, creating lightless passages through boulders and along the canyon bottom. The most extensive talus caves have active streams, which create additional cave passages by eroding the bedrock below the boulders. Talus caves form in many types of rocks. They often follow fault lines. Only a few small talus caves have formed in Sequoia and Kings Canyon National Parks. Excellent examples can be found at Pinnacles National Monument in central California.

Other Types of Caves in California

☐ LAVA TUBES

■ SEA CAVES

☐ TALUS CAVES

▨ LIMESTONE CAVES

■ MUD CAVES

5

Right:
Stalactites and a stalagmite over a floor of white rimstone. During spring months when the cave is wettest, these small rimstone pools are filled with acidic water that has seeped into the cave from above.

Below:
The large, natural entrance to Crystal Cave lies at the base of a small cliff at the bottom of Cascade Creek's canyon. This opening was first discovered by two fishermen in 1918.

The entrance to Crystal Cave now sits twenty feet above Cascade Creek, but once the creek bed lay above the entry passage. As the rushing waters erode the stream bed, they deepen the canyon. Long ago, the stream cut into a cave passage filled with groundwater. Eventually, the canyon cut through this passage, opening and creating the cave entrance.

Just inside is the Spider Web Gate, constructed by creative Park Service employees and installed by the Civilian Conservation Corps more than fifty years ago. A steady, cool breeze flows from the entrance on warm days, making this a comfortable spot to wait for your tour of the cave to begin.

Tours start with a brief introduction. Then your guide swings open the historic gate and you begin a fifty-minute journey into a different world.

Inside, many strangely shaped cave formations—known as *speleothems*—adorn the walls, ceilings and floors. Composed of the mineral calcite, they form very slowly. The most well-known speleothems are the *stalactites* that hang down from the ceiling or ledges, and *stalagmites* that grow upward from the floor.

Ahead, the sound of running water grows louder as you approach a bridge across the cave stream. The water has cut a channel into marble bedrock, exposing the rock's blue-gray and white banding. Crystal Cave lies entirely within marble, but in most places sediments and deposits hide the rock's true color.

In the past, lateral movements of the stream to the right of the bridge cut a series of horizontal ledges into the wall. Look for finger-sized, curled and bent calcite deposits hanging from the underside of the ledges.

These formations, called *helectites,* are (like all speleothems) created by weak carbonic acid and water.

This natural acid, a mixture of carbon dioxide and water, slowly dissolves marble. Dilute carbonic acid, percolating through marble or other calcium-rich rocks, dissolves small amounts of the stone. When the acid mixture seeps into an open cave passage, some of the dissolved minerals *precipitate*—solidify out of the solution—creating formations such as the uneven helectites.

Deeper in the cave the passage narrows as it runs through an area of dark, erosion-resistant stone called *schist.* Schist is formed from ancient seafloor deposits of silt and clay compressed and changed over millions of years into hard stone, then lifted up as part of the Sierra Nevada. This narrow passage marks where marble, long since cut away by the stream, once lay between the schist.

Mineral-laden acidic water, dripping from the ceiling onto the cave floor, created a group of stalagmites here. In building the trail, workers shifted a block of these formations a few inches. Now slightly off center from the water dripping from above, new calcite deposits form on the sides of the stalagmites, instead of at their tips.

The cave widens again in the Junction Room—the first stop on most tours. Here, your guide will begin to explain the cave's features and formations. This is the best place to observe the stream. Slow-moving water

Above:
A visitor enjoys cave curtains in the Curtain Room. This small room is the first of many rooms containing cave formations along the cave trail in the middle levels of Crystal Cave.

Right:
A visitor ascends the stairs at the bottom of the Little Cathedral Room. This is the tallest room in the cave with a ceiling nearly one hundred feet above the cave trail.

deposits silt and sand over marble bedrock in the pool by the trail. The trail leaves the stream here. Past this point, passages near the stream are small, muddy and hard to follow.

Two-hundred feet upstream, several large boulders hoisted, creating a small cave. A jumble of broken rocks the passage along the stream. [...]cave, other winding, twisting passages provide access to sections of the creek. The stream is first seen in the most northerly reaches of Crystal Cave's passages, hundreds of feet beyond the trail.

Past the Junction Room, the trail climbs to an upper-level of the cave. The original route followed small, narrow passages until workers enlarged this section by the late 1940s. Blasting revealed pockets of fragile crystals. Some contain tan-colored, half-inch crystals of *aragonite*. Others bear translucent, quarter-inch crystals of aptly named *dog tooth spar*.

In the fifty years since these passages were enlarged, new cave formations have started to grow. Soda-straw stalactites have sprouted from the ceiling, and a half-inch curtain-like formation hangs on a section of cave wall.

Their size gives an idea of the rate at which cave formations develop. But their rate of growth varies dramatically, depending on conditions in the cave. The amount of acidic water flowing across a formation's surface, the water's chemistry and many other factors act to speed or slow the process. Formations may stop growing altogether for a time, then start again. This makes it hard to tell the age of any formation by size alone. Geologists must sample formations and compare their chemistry with the expected composition for calcite. Through the slow release of radiation, rocks change through time. By measuring how much a rock has changed, geologists can estimate how old it is. It's a technique used selectively, since sampling a formation usually means destroying it.

A variety of formations decorate the upper-level rooms in this part of Crystal Cave. Curtain-like formations hang over the trail in the Curtain Room, the first and smallest of the upper-level rooms on the trail. Curtains form as acidic groundwater, carrying dissolved minerals, runs down the cave wall, depositing thin sheets of calcite. Many small stalactites decorate the ceiling, adding to the room's beauty and complexity.

An arched ceiling and large curtains resembling a pipe organ lie further up the trail in the Organ Room. Notice the broken curtains. Some were damaged in 1957 when tours were unguided, and in 1991 two people left a large tour and broke several square feet of curtain. Vandalism and souvenir hunting have permanently scarred these formations, robbing us all of the chance to experience their original beauty.

A series of shallow pools on the right marks the beginning of the Dome Room. The low calcite walls that hold the water in the pools are a formation known as *rimstone dams*. They form where water collects on a flat surface. Calcite precipitates from the acidic water, forming a rim of rock around the edges of the pools.

Many stalactites hang from above. To the left stands a large stalagmite that resembles the Capitol Dome in Washington, D.C. Beneath the stalagmite lies an expanse of *flowstone*. Flowstone forms where acidic water rich in dissolved calcite flows over a surface, slowly depositing a smooth layer of calcite. All these formations have grown from a single crack in the ceiling where groundwater seeps into the Dome Room.

On the right wall is an oddly shaped pendant of rough, dark rock resembling a group of stalactites. Yet, unlike stalactites and other *speleothems* that grew in the cave, this is a piece of the original marble that didn't dissolve away as the room formed. Remnants like these are called *primary formations*, or *speleogens*.

The Pipe Organ formation in the Organ Room. Early explorers believed this formation of calcite flowstone and cave curtains resembled a pipe organ and named this room of the cave for the formation. The Organ has been severely damaged since the cave was opened to the public. (See the Cave Conservation section for more details.)

Since 1987, when the trail was paved, there's been a slow transformation in the Dome Room. Formations that looked drab gray in prior years appear sparkling white again. Before paving, visitors stirred up dust from the cave trail which then settled on formations, dulling their beauty. Now, as new rock coats the formations (through the same processes that first built them), the layers of dust are covered by fresh calcite. The increased flow of water after the wet winter of 1992-1993 sped the process and brightened formations in more than a dozen places throughout the cave.

The next passage is called "Fat Man's Misery." More fun than misery, this narrow section requires that all but small children turn sideways to slip through.

A caver moves through the top of a canyon passage between the Dome Room and the Shield Room on the Wild Tour route.

Just past this challenge, you enter the openness of Marble Hall: the largest room in Crystal Cave. One-hundred-fifty feet long and forty feet wide, its arched ceiling rises sixty feet overhead in places.

Some of the largest and most colorful formations in Crystal Cave, including curtains, stalactites and stalagmites, grow from the room's right wall and adjacent ceiling. A thin band of schist covers the wall near the observation platform. Deposits of unusual minerals—including aragonite crystals, gypsum, a soft mineral named hydromagnesite and calcite formations shaped like raised bubbles or blisters—dot the schist.

A pile of broken stone covers the floor of Marble Hall. The rocks probably fell from the ceiling during the cave's formation. Such collapses, called *breakdown,* happen most often where ceilings are weaker, such as in large rooms, where passages intersect and near cave entrances.

All tours stop here, allowing visitors time to take in the size and visual wonders of Marble Hall. The hall is also a good place to experience the true nature of caves. If tour members feel comfortable, the guide may turn out the lights for a time to introduce them to the total darkness of a natural cave environment.

Leaving Marble Hall, the trail enters a man-made tunnel that runs thirty feet to the Fault Room. Repeated drilling and blasting during construction in the 1930s created tons of rubble. Trail builders dumped the debris on the floor of the Fault Room. In the process, they broke formations and filled and covered passages—completely altering this section of cave. What seemed convenient then is seen as a blunder now. Long-term management plans call for the removal of this material.

The tallest passages and rooms in Crystal Cave lie between Marble Hall and the trail's return to the Junction Room. The Fault Room is seventy feet tall, and the ceiling in the Little Cathedral Room soars more than one-hundred feet above the trail. Many curtains and stalactites grow from these tall walls and flat ceilings. Small ledges high on the walls lead to passages with speleothems, reflective pools and dramatic views of the trail far below.

Following the trail down on the return to the Junction Room, you again begin to hear the cave stream. From the Junction Room, your group retraces its route along the stream to Spider Web Gate. Your journey through Crystal Cave is over. But the memories of beautiful, strangely shaped formations, delicate crystals, large subterranean rooms and a flowing cave stream remain. Perhaps they'll lure you back to Crystal Cave again, or lead you to discover the charms of other caves.

A cave guide discusses aspects of Crystal Cave with visitors in Marble Hall.

2

PEOPLE AND CRYSTAL CAVE

The erosive force of Cascade Creek opened the Spider Web Gate entrance to Crystal Cave tens of thousands of years ago. No one knows how many changes the surrounding area went through before Native Americans first discovered the cave. No one knows how they used the cave. We have only a few clues to their presence.

In 1990, Park employees discovered small pieces of charred wood partly imbedded in the calcite of a rimstone dam fifty feet inside the Spider Web Gate. How did it get there? An animal may have carried in wood charred by a forest fire. Or perhaps someone using the cave for shelter built a fire here. Researchers collected and dated a small sample of wood. The wood dates to between 1700 and 1850 A.D.—a time during which Native Americans lived in the area.

Was Crystal Cave home or shelter for early peoples? Was the cave a sacred site? These pieces of wood raise many questions that may never be fully answered.

Hale Tharp was the first European-American to explore this area in the late 1850s. However, it wasn't until 1918, twenty-eight years after the creation of Sequoia National Park, that European-Americans discovered Crystal Cave.

There were few high-country backpacking trails prior to the 1930s; hikers often followed the Black Oak Trail and other lower-elevation routes near Crystal Cave. Two ranger stations operated near the cave during this time: the Colony Mill Station on the original road into the Park, and the Hidden Springs Station on a tributary of the North Fork. Low-elevation streams and rivers, including Cascade Creek, were stocked with trout during these early Park years.

On April 28, 1918, two park trail construction employees—Cassius Monroe Webster and Alex L. Medley—were fishing for newly stocked trout in Cascade Creek about a mile below the Black Oak Trail. They discovered the entrance and felt the cool breeze flowing from it. They reported their find to Park Superintendent Walter Fry.

Fry, a caving enthusiast, had explored at least four other caves in the Park by 1918. He took an immediate interest in this discovery and apparently led the first exploration party into the cave two days later, on April 30.

Fry described the Park's caves in a bulletin written in 1925 for the Park nature guide service. Of Crystal Cave he wrote:

"It is in this cave that nature has lavishly traced her design in decorative glory. Throughout the entire cave the stalactite formations are rich and wonderfully varied in size, form and color. In some of the chambers the ceiling is a mass of stalactites, some very large, others tapering down to needle points. Others drop down from the roof great folds of massive draperies, while in yet others are great fluted columns of stalagmites of surpassing symmetry and beauty."

Fry had a barricade and door placed at the entrance to the cave. On May 6, he wrote to the Director of the National Park Service, Stephen Mather, informing him of the discovery and suggesting that the cave be commercialized. Mather's response came in two letters, one in May, and another in October 1918. He suggested that the cave entrance be blocked with "lumber sufficiently strong that

Opposite page:
Historic photo believed to have been taken approximately one week after Crystal Cave was discovered in 1918. This section of the cave along the stream is only one hundred and fifty feet inside the cave entrance. The current trail passes directly through this area.

Cave Conservation

Left:
An early photo of the Pipe Organ formation as it appeared when the cave was discovered.

Top, middle:
Recent photo showing the broken curtains at the bottom of the Organ. They were broken in 1957 and again in 1991, permanently altering the Organ.

Bottom, middle:
Contemporary photo showing the Fairy Pools and the stalactite and column formations adjacent to them. Notice the shortened length of many stalactites and the missing columns. The white deposits on the ends of the broken formations are new growth that has formed since the stalactites were broken in 1957.

Far right:
An early photo of the Fairy Pools showing the formations around the pools as they appeared prior to 1957.

Since Crystal Cave's discovery, the Park Service has worked to protect its formations and wildlife. But inappropriate development in the 1930s and the thoughtless actions and vandalism of a few visitors have altered the cave and destroyed some of its original beauty. Hundreds of formations lie broken, many more stand discolored with layers of dirt and dust. Hundreds of tons of blast rubble litters passages along the cave trail. We may never fully know the effect our actions have had on the cave's sensitive wildlife.

Armed now with a better understanding of caves, the Park works to prevent further damage to Crystal Cave and, where possible, to repair the damage already done. The Park took an important step in 1992, by limiting to 70 (down from 140) the number of people on any tour group. Before 1988, guides sometimes led groups of more than two-hundred people. Such large groups were difficult to control and impossible to fully monitor in delicate areas of the cave.

Fragile formations near the trail frequently suffer damage or break when touched. Rock walls and hand rails may be built to protect them while still allowing them to be seen from the trail. Tests have shown that many soiled formations can be rinsed clean with water, opening the way to full-scale restoration efforts. Other work indicates that blast rubble, left from the enlargement of passages during the cave's development, can be removed without further damaging the cave.

The restoration of Crystal Cave by the Park Service depends on the efforts of volunteers. The work proceeds slowly and carefully. Additional restoration and management techniques will be developed and their effects on the cave evaluated. Future visitors will see a rejuvenated Crystal Cave: shining with more of its original beauty, and perhaps a healthier community of cave animals.

If caves protected within our National Parks suffer damage, how have other caves fared? Often poorly. All across our country, people have stripped caves of their formations and artifacts, reducing them to empty holes. Groundwater pollution and the destruction and disturbance of cave habitats have driven many cave animals to the edge of extinction. Many species of cave-dwelling wildlife, including three species of bats, make up a significant proportion of our country's threatened and endangered animals.

Caves, like all aspects of the natural world, are under siege from the ever-growing burden of human population, and the pollution that follows. The protection of caves around the world will be a difficult challenge, both now and far into the future. The fate of their special features and inhabitants remains uncertain.

no one can break through." He also instructed Superintendent Fry to restrict access to the cave. He indicated a personal concern for the well-being of this Park feature, stating: "I am not going to take a chance of any injury to this cave until we can... handle it in the right way." By 1921 a strong, locked gate was in place.

In these early years, important visitors—congressmen and local civic leaders granted permission by the Superintendent—toured the cave. Rangers oversaw visits, which required a four-mile round-trip hike from Colony Mill Road. Entrance was through a door in Fry's barricade. Kerosene lanterns and miners' lamps lit the way. Without a formal trail, the route was muddy and slick and sometimes small and constricted.

In August of 1926, after a visit by congressman Phil Swing, Superintendent John R. White allowed trips into the cave as far as the Junction Room. Director Mather intervened and closed the cave again on September 25. Despite these difficulties and restrictions some people did visit the cave during the 1920s and the early 1930s. Tours were conducted for Boy Scout troops, residents of the town of Three Rivers and summer Park visitors staying in Giant Forest. Others entered the cave illegally, sometimes vandalizing and destroying cave formations.

Development of the cave finally began in 1938. Congressman Albert E. Carter, from Three Rivers, sponsored an addition to the Interior Department Appropriations Bill, specifically providing $55,000 to develop Crystal Cave for visitors.

During the 1930s, extensive development work took place throughout the Park. The economic hardships of the Depression left millions of Americans unemployed, and President Franklin D. Roosevelt responded with the creation of government-sponsored work programs. In the National Parks, the Civilian Conservation Corps (CCC) provided thousands of men for a huge variety of projects and developments.

At Sequoia, CCC workers constructed facilities in Giant Forest, completed the Generals Highway, built campgrounds and, beginning in 1938, helped develop Crystal Cave.

In the summer of that year approximately forty men from a CCC company, based in Potwisha Camp (now the site of Potwisha Campground), began work on the cave. They lived within the cave's entrance and below the cave in a clearing at the junction of Cascade and Yucca creeks. They installed Spider Web Gate, built restrooms and a water system. They worked on the trail and enlarged passages between the Junction and Curtain rooms, between the Organ Room and the Dome Room and between Marble Hall and the Fault Room. They also installed a lighting system with more than one-hundred incandescent bulbs.

Some aspects of this development stirred controversy. Some local businessmen believed that a road to the cave was an essential part of the development. Some Park employees opposed the road, believing that the four-mile round-trip walk gave visitors an excellent opportunity to see the surrounding area. Congress eventually funded the road, which was completed in the spring of 1941.

Developers also debated the merits of hydroelectric versus generator-supplied electricity. There was only enough money for one power source. A generator was chosen and installed in a room adjacent to the restrooms.

In May of 1940, the cave opened for tours. Fifteen-thousand people made the four-mile hike to visit Crystal Cave that first year. In a press release announcing the closure of the cave for the season on September 8, Park Superintendent E. T. Scoyen stated, "I am greatly pleased with the respect shown the delicate formations by all these visitors, as not a single stalactite or stalagmite has been damaged [this year]."

After being open three summers, Crystal Cave remained closed for three years during World War II. Since reopening in 1946, the number of visitors steadily increased each

year through the 1960s. On its busiest day, the Saturday of Labor Day weekend in 1968, the cave saw more than two-thousand visitors.

Through the 1970s and 1980s, some sixty-thousand people visited Crystal Cave each year. On holidays and busy August weekends more than fifteen-hundred people a day entered the cave.

In 1982, due to an increasingly tighter budget, the National Park Service decided to end cave tours conducted by park employees. The Park Service signed an agreement with the Sequoia Natural History Association (SNHA), a nonprofit educational organization, to continue offering cave tours to the public. Natural History Associations exist for many of our National Parks and Monuments. They traditionally sell books, sponsor seminars and provide support for Park educational programs.

The SNHA provides a stable, self-supporting, economic base for operating the cave. The cave is open seven days a week during busy summer months. The Association initiated special tours including candlelight and geology tours, weekend tours during May and September and a Wild Cave Tour program.

In 1984, private contractors installed a new lighting system for the cave using modern fluorescent, quartz-halogen and mercury-vapor lights. Following this work, in the spring of 1985, members of the California Conservation Corps paved the original packed-dirt cave trail with concrete.

Starting in 1992, through an agreement with the Park Service, the SNHA reduced tour sizes to a maximum of seventy people. This effort has helped to protect the cave's resources while providing higher-quality tours to visitors.

Crystal Cave is one of California's more popular commercial caves. As more is learned of the cave in the years ahead, further changes may be required as the National Park Service strives to protect this precious, yet fragile, site.

Top:
In the geologic process known as subduction, dense oceanic plates such as those beneath the Pacific Ocean may slide beneath a less dense continental plate such as North America, and be forced downward into the Earth's molten mantle. When rock and sediment from the old ocean floor reach the mantle it melts in the intense heat of the Earth's interior.

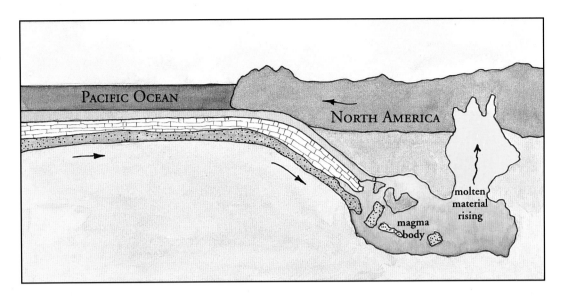

Middle:
The floor of the ancient Pacific as it may have looked 200 million years ago. Depicted are crinoids (lower left corner and background), bryozoans (left side), brachiopods (lower right and lower center), straight and coiled cephlapods (center and lower center), starfish, snails (lower center), sponges (far right and upper left corner) and trilobites (lower right corner). The calcium-rich remains of these animals were deposited as reefs and sediments. Some of the reef material was subducted, while other reef deposits were deeply buried along the western edge on North America and were transformed into limestone and finally marble.

Bottom:
The ocean bottom that is subducted beneath the continental plate is often a complex mixture of sediments, rock, and animal remains previously laid down in roughly horizontal layers.

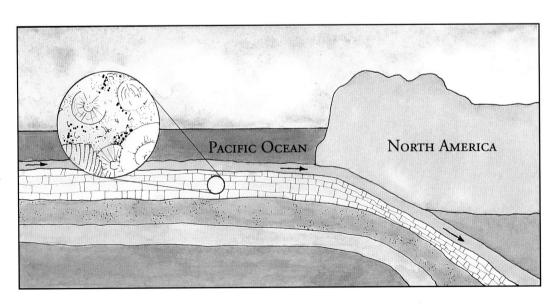

3

CAVE GEOLOGY

The geologic history of Crystal Cave began some 200 million years ago on the floor of an ancient sea—an ancestor of today's Pacific Ocean.

The Earth's surface, including the seafloor, consists of a number of immense crustal plates. The plates move slowly but constantly. Like slow-motion bumper cars, they may collide head-on, scrape alongside each other or pull apart.

Dense oceanic plates formed the floor of the ancient sea. The land to the east was part of the lighter, continental North American Plate. Over millions of years, this plate has collided with the denser oceanic plates, which often slid beneath the continent of North America—a process called subduction. The relentless force of the collision and the resulting *subduction* spawned earthquakes, undersea landslides, volcanic eruptions and broke the earth's crust, lifting it to form mountain ranges.

Animals, many known today only from fossils, flourished in the shallow, ancient sea. Ammonites with whorled shells and crab-like trilobites scurried among thickets of corals, coral-like bryozoa and the feathery arms of crinoid sea stars. Myriad small radiolarians and foraminiferans—types of marine protozoans——swarmed through the water.

Many of these animals created shells or skeletons of calcium carbonate. When individuals died, their shells and skeletons remained, accumulating over generations into rocky reefs. The chemistry of warm ocean water also led to a build-up of sediments rich in calcium. Over millennia, new reefs grew over older ones, and volcanoes and undersea landslides periodically buried reefs and sediments.

The weight of layer on layer of rock and sediment compacted and dried the older deposits and eventually transformed them into fossil-rich limestone or other types of rock such as shale and sandstone.

Two-hundred-million years ago, all the land on Earth was part of a single, vast super-continent, Pangaea. Around one-hundred-fifty-million years ago Pangaea began to

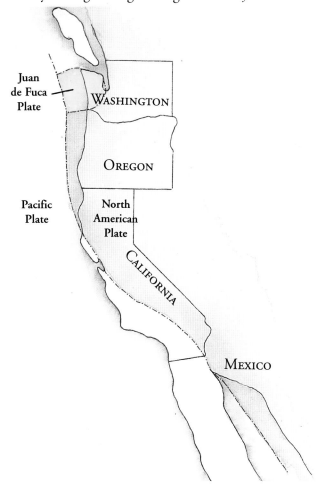

THE MAKING OF MARBLE AND MOUNTAINS

The boundaries of three of the Earth's gigantic crustal plates lie along the western edge of the United States. It was the slow but relentless movement of these plates that created the Sierra Nevada and directly influenced the development of Crystal Cave.

CRYSTAL CAVE MAP LEGEND

— CAVE TRAIL AND PLATFORMS

- - - WILD TOUR ROUTE

~~~ CREEKS AND POOLS

STALACTITES AND STALAGMITES

SHIELDS AND HELECTITES

FLOWSTONE AND RIMSTONE

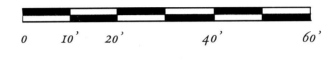

0   10'   20'   40'   60'

GATE

10' CEILING

1' CEILING

SPIDER WEB
ENTRANCE

CAVE STREAM
RESURGENCE

SUGAR COOKIE ROOM

6' CEILING

3' CEILING

ENSANTINA
ENTRANCE

GATE

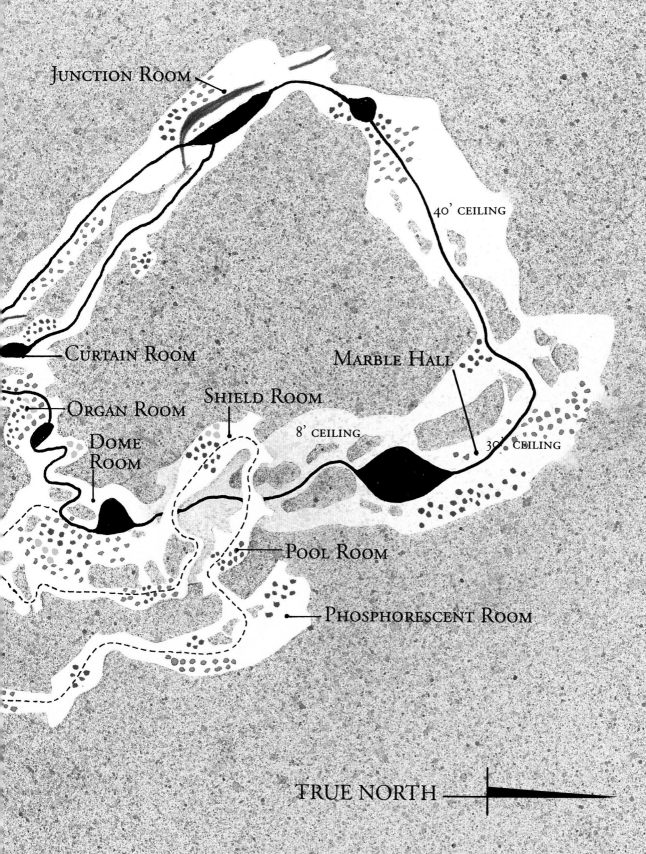

JUNCTION ROOM

40' CEILING

CURTAIN ROOM

MARBLE HALL

ORGAN ROOM

SHIELD ROOM

DOME
ROOM

8' CEILING

30' CEILING

POOL ROOM

PHOSPHORESCENT ROOM

TRUE NORTH

Top:
A view of the boundary area of North America and the Pacific Ocean about 150 million to 100 million years ago. Geologists believe that ancient ocean deposits on the edge of North America were metamorphosed or changed during this time. Siltstone and shale became schist, sandstone changed to quartzite and limestone transformed into marble. The heat and pressure that caused the ocean-deposited rocks to metamorphose came from upwelling magma, which eventually cooled into the granitic rocks that form most of the Sierra Nevada today.

Middle:
Twenty five million years ago the metamorphic rocks and the granitic rocks cooled from magma were uplifted to become the Sierra Nevada. The incredible pressures that caused the mountains to rise also caused volcanoes to erupt and other mountain ranges in Nevada and other Western States to form. As the mountain ranges were uplifted they became exposed to the erosive power of wind, water, and glacial ice.

Bottom:
The Sierra Nevada today, with extensive glacial valleys and only a few remnant pieces of metamorphic rock remaining. Most of the metamorphic rock was eroded long ago. Some of the remaining metamorphic rock is marble. Crystal Cave has formed in one of these bodies of stone.

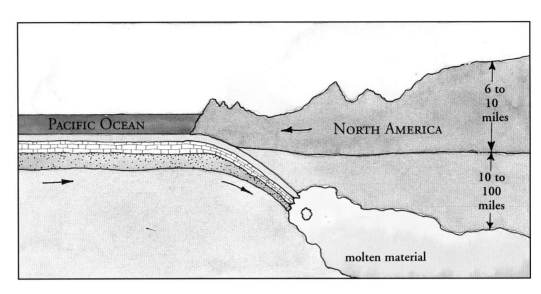

PACIFIC OCEAN   NORTH AMERICA

6 to 10 miles

10 to 100 miles

molten material

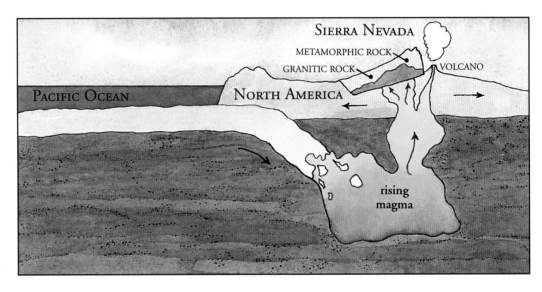

SIERRA NEVADA
METAMORPHIC ROCK
GRANITIC ROCK
VOLCANO
PACIFIC OCEAN   NORTH AMERICA
rising magma

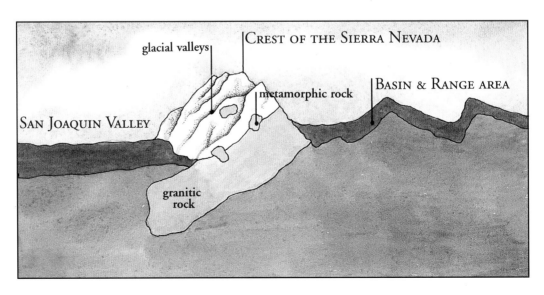

glacial valleys   CREST OF THE SIERRA NEVADA

metamorphic rock   BASIN & RANGE area

SAN JOAQUIN VALLEY

granitic rock

break apart as North America and Europe separated. The intense pressures and geologic activity within the Earth led to further changes in marine deposits. The ocean floor melted as it slid into the Earth's mantle beneath the moving continental plate. Vast amounts of molten rock, *magma,* moved upward through the crust sometimes creating volcanoes on the surface. In other places, magma invaded and altered marine rocks through tremendous heat and pressure.

Sandstone and other sandy sediments became quartzite. Basalt and ancient lava became meta-volcanic rock. Siltstone and shale became schist. The limestones became the blue-and-white-banded marble in which Crystal Cave formed. The magma eventually cooled and solidified to become the granite, diorite and other igneous (solidified from magma) rocks that make up much of the Sierra Nevada today.

The metamorphic rocks (those changed from one form to another) of the Sierra remained buried for millions of years. The Pacific oceanic plates and the North American Plate continued to collide. Twenty-five-million years ago, the North American Plate met the East Pacific Rise, an area of volcanic activity and spreading between two plates on the ocean floor, and new pressures developed. Part of the western edge of North America broke away and began moving north, creating the San Andreas Fault. Volcanoes erupted throughout the area. To the east, the Earth's crust fractured and stretched, thrusting huge pieces of crust upward—forming the mountain ranges of Nevada and Southern California. Sequoia National Park sits on a small section of one immense block that lifted thousands of feet to become the Sierra Nevada.

The rocks in the uplifted pieces of crust were broken and fractured as the mountains slowly rose. The forces of wind, water and glacial ice eroded the broken stone, creating canyons and jagged peaks. Overlying volcanic and ocean-deposited rocks eroded away and now fill valleys at the base of the Sierra Nevada with deep layers of mud, sand, gravel and stones. This process exposed the underlying granitic core of the Sierra and these rocks make up most of the mountain range today.

In some places, the ocean-born schist and marble did not erode, remaining instead as *roof pendants,* remnants of the rocks that roofed the magma and granite of the Sierra. Today, these metamorphic rocks survive as small pendants capping a tremendous volume of granitic rock. Crystal Cave formed in one of these marble pendants.

Above:
Cave pearls formed in a
shallow rimstone pool near
the cave's entrance.

Right:
A row of formations in the
Phosphorescent Room

Each cave is unique: its size and shape, the formations it holds and its natural history determined by the complex interplay of natural influences and circumstances. But caves share common attributes, too.

The location and size of masses of carbonate rocks such as marble and limestone determine the location and size of caves. Within these rocks, caves are defined by the entry and exit points of the acidic water that creates them.

The formation of Crystal Cave began as Yucca and Cascade creeks scoured away overlying rocks to expose the marble which contains the cave. The creeks carried a gritty load of rock eroded from the mountain which increased their erosive power. This erosion is an on-going process.

The marble pendant that holds Crystal Cave is small: roughly three-hundred feet long. Exposed to a height of three-hundred feet in Cascade Creek canyon and two-hundred feet in the shallower Yucca Creek valley, the block of marble creates a seven-hundred-foot-wide ridge separating the two creeks. Deposits of reddish mica-schist flank it on either side. A deposit of once-molten granitic rock sits one-thousand feet above the cave, near the bridge across Cascade Creek.

The glaciers that eroded higher slopes never reached this low-elevation valley, but other kinds of erosion, including chemical erosion, ate away at the marble.

This type of chemical erosion begins when carbon dioxide gas, found in air and soil, combines with water to form carbonic acid. Carbonic acid is common in the environment; it's what gives soda and beer their "fizz" and seltzer water its mildly bitter taste. It's a weak acid, but still strong enough to dissolve carbonate rocks like marble. Acidic groundwater seeping through cracks and fractures in the marble slowly, but steadily, widened them.

The chemical power of carbonic acid and the scouring force of underground streams carved the passageways and rooms of Crystal Cave inside the marble.

Some cave streams form from the accumulation of many small tributaries. Others, called *sinking streams*, form when a surface stream erodes its way into a cave passage and is diverted to a subterranean route.

The Crystal Cave stream flows from the cave through a narrow canyon beneath the cave entrance to join Cascade Creek. In the cave, it runs through the entrance passage and the Junction Room, beneath the Fault Room, and into small passages of broken rock hundreds of feet beyond Marble Hall, nearly beneath Yucca Creek valley. This large, isolated valley is usually dry below the marble pendant bearing Crystal Cave. Water from Yucca Creek currently appears to form a sinking stream, captured by the cave to flow underground to become the Crystal Cave stream.

The cave walls tell the story of water flow through the cave. Acidic water creates scallops or pock-marks where it flows turbulently across a surface. The scallops give clues to the water's source and direction. The steep face on the end of a scallop forms in the direction the water was flowing. Smaller scallops indicate faster-moving water.

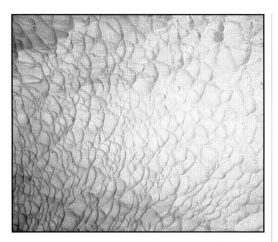

Scallops formed in a cave wall by turbulent, flowing water. These shallow depressions are one-half to four inches across.

From the ridge above the dry canyon of Yucca Creek, a sheer vertical pit drops into the large, dusty passages of Crystal Cave. The water that cut these tunnels also came from Yucca Creek. Scallops in these passages reveal that water flowed rapidly down through this part of the cave into the area near Marble Hall. The scallops, the location of the openings and the structure of the passage indicate that in the past, as now, the primary source of the cave's water was Yucca Creek.

Speleogens

A flow of acidic groundwater slowly dissolves and erodes rock. Sometimes, through a process called *differential erosion*, a few rough, oddly-shaped pieces or protrusions survive as the surrounding rock is eaten away. Called *primary formations* or *speleogens*, these marble or schist remnants were probably less soluble and more erosion-resistant, or may have been exposed to a smaller flow of water than the rock around them. Primary formations can be found in most caves but they are particularly common in Crystal Cave. Look for these stone remnants on the ceiling of the Junction Room, in the Organ Room and along the walls of the Dome Room and Marble Hall.

Geologists believe that the source of water and carbonic acid, what they call a cave's *recharge,* plays a key role in shaping the pattern of a cave's rooms and passages.

There are several common types of recharge for caves.

• In some, water seeps down into the cave through overlying layers of sandstone or other porous rock.

• Other caves are formed by acidic or thermal water rising up from a water source below the cave.

• In another type of recharge, water may enter a cave from surface depressions called *sinkholes*. In this case, the amount of water moving through the cave remains relatively constant over time.

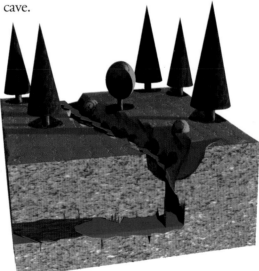

• Finally, as is the case with Crystal Cave, a sinking stream may serve as a water source, with tremendous variation in the amount of water entering the cave system, over time.

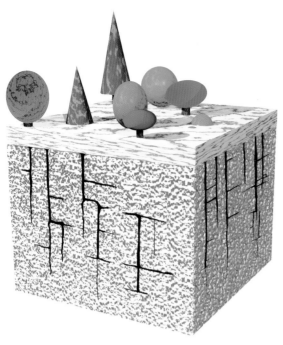

Illustration 1
Vertical and horizontal fractures form in rock due to internal pressures and stress from within the earth. Acidic water may seep into these cracks and begin the process of cave development.

The original shape, direction and character of the fractures will strongly influence the final shape and nature of the cave that forms.

Illustration 2
Acidic ground water may also follow bedding planes. Bedding planes develop between layers of sediments that later harden into stone. Caves formed along the planes take on a particular shape and pattern based

upon the shape and pattern of the bedding planes. Generally these horizontal layers only exist in sedimentary rocks such as limestone where no intense mountain building has occurred.

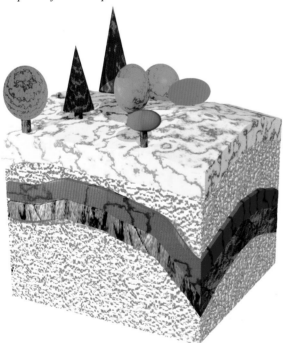

Illustration 3
Exfoliation occurs in metamorphic and igneous rocks which have surfaced from deep beneath the Earth. These types of rock are generally found in the mountains.

Erosion removes the overlying layers of stone and sediment, and eliminates a tremendous weight upon the rock. With this weight removed, the rock stretches slightly and breaks, often in

long curved lines parallel to the Earth's surface. These breaks in the rock are another route that acidic water can follow to create a cave. Crystal Cave was formed in this manner.

Illustration 4
Sometimes the acidic water that creates caves also produces openings by moving through the small pores and spaces found between the grains and crystals of a rock.

These openings have shapes and patterns based on the shape of those small pores, and create a specific type of cave passage.

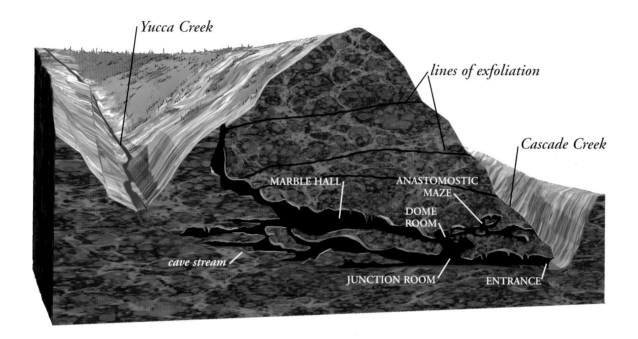

The other important factor in determining the patterns of a cave's passages is *porosity*—the type of naturally occurring spaces, openings and weaknesses within the rock. There are three main types of porosity involved in cave development:
• vertical and horizontal fractures within the rock;
• pores or spaces among the rock's grains or crystals; and
• seams that exist between layers of rock are called *bedding partings. Exfoliation separations* occur where rock has flexed upward after being freed from the weight of overlying rock.

This last type of porosity applies to Crystal Cave. Bedding partings occur in roughly horizontal bands in limestone between layers of the sediments from which the rock formed. Exfoliation happens when an overlying layer of stone erodes away, allowing

the rocks beneath to flex and break, often in long curved layers parallel to the ground surface. Exfoliations appear in marble and other metamorphic rock, as well as in igneous rocks, such as granite.

The porosity of a rock, combined with the type of recharge in a cave system combine to produce a specific type of cave passage. In Crystal Cave, a sinking stream with variable rate of flow and porous, exfoliated rock, have created a system of winding, interconnected passages known to geologists as an *anastomotic maze.*

In Crystal Cave, a well-developed anastomotic maze called the Catacombs runs parallel to the historic Spider Web Gate entrance. Three levels of low, horizontal tunnels meander through bedrock in a pattern like a braided surface stream. The Catacombs' passages meet in junctions and intersections. Similar mazes occur in most

31

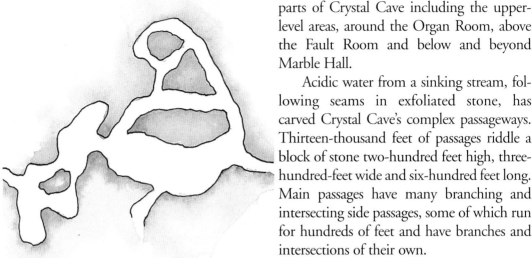

A map of a small section of the Catacombs area of Crystal Cave. The winding, interconnected passages of the Catacombs are an example of an anastomotic maze. Much of Crystal Cave is this type of cave passage.

parts of Crystal Cave including the upper-level areas, around the Organ Room, above the Fault Room and below and beyond Marble Hall.

Acidic water from a sinking stream, following seams in exfoliated stone, has carved Crystal Cave's complex passageways. Thirteen-thousand feet of passages riddle a block of stone two-hundred feet high, three-hundred-feet wide and six-hundred feet long. Main passages have many branching and intersecting side passages, some of which run for hundreds of feet and have branches and intersections of their own.

The Chemistry of Groundwater

Groundwater dissolves marble through a chemical process involving *ions*—atoms or molecules with a positive or negative electrical charge. Ions combine with other ions with opposite charges to form compounds and minerals. As water (H_2O), in the form of rain or melted snow, percolates through the soil above the cave, it combines with carbon dioxide (CO_2), a byproduct of the organisms living in the soil. Together they create carbonic acid, (H_2CO_3)—a combination of a positively charged hydrogen ion, (H^{+1}) and a negatively charged bicarbonate ion (HCO_3^{-1}). Inside cracks in the rocks, the hydrogen ions react with the marble, which is made of calcite, ($CaCO_3$). The calcite slowly dissolves and is carried away with water seeping through the rock, creating open cave passages. Chemists and geologists represent these reactions as formulas:

The arrows with points on each end indicate these reactions flow both ways. In one direction, the reactions lead to the dissolving of calcite rock. In the other, they create calcite cave formations.

As acidic water saturated with dissolved calcite seeps through the bedrock into the air-filled spaces of the cave, much of the carbon dioxide in it bubbles away. This weakens the carbonic acid. The weaker acid solution can't hold as much dissolved calcium carbonate, so some precipitates out as calcite rock. This simple chemical reaction—repeated countless times through hundreds of thousands of years—can build massive cave formations.

$$CO_2 + H_2O \leftrightarrow H_2CO_3$$

which ionizes to $H^{+1} + HCO_3^{-1}$

$$CaCO_3 + 2H^{+1} \leftrightarrow H_2O + CO_2 + Ca^{+2}$$

Caves occur in two distinct zones beneath the surface of the Earth. Passages formed in one zone can be different in appearance and shape from those in the other. The level of the water table, which may change over time, divides and defines these zones.

Some cave passages develop below the level of the water table, in what is known as the *phreatic zone.* Acidic water fills the pores, spaces and cracks in the rock, and cave passages form underwater as carbonic acid dissolves the marble. Rooms and passages which form in this zone are often rounded and vary in size from small to enormous. Most of Crystal Cave appears to have formed in this zone. The Junction Room, Organ Room, Dome Room, Marble Hall and the passages between them formed in this way.

Caves which begin forming underwater are often left dry as the surrounding water table sinks. Surface streams lie at the top of the water table. As they erode rock and soil, they lower their valley floor—and with it, the water table in the nearby ridges. When the water table drops far enough, the cave drains. Sometimes, due to changes in climate or hydrology, or to glacial advance, the water table may rise and submerge the cave again.

A drained cave passage lies in the *vadose zone*—the area above the water table. Even though most of a cave has drained, cave streams may continue flowing in lower cave passages. Free-flowing streams, moving across the floor of an underground passage erode rock just as surface streams do. They often carve narrow passages with tall, rough, canyonlike walls.

An example of this kind of passage can be seen inside the cave entrance. The stream has cut a narrow channel beneath the first bridge along the cave trail.

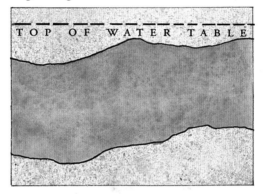

Top:
A developing cave passage in the phreatic zone below the water table.

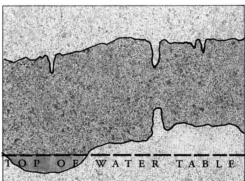

Middle:
A mostly drained cave passage in the vadose zone. The flowing water in the lower right may continue to create new cave passages by acting as a down-cutting surface stream. Passages formed in this way often resemble canyons.

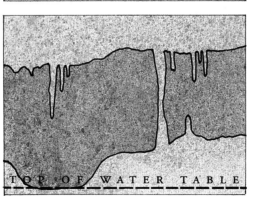

Bottom:
A dry cave passage. Often passageways of this type are called fossil passages because they were created by extinct or fossil water flow patterns. Generally these passages are in the upper level of a cave and change only through the slow development of cave formations.

The formation of rooms and the enlargement of fractures marked a final stage in the creation of Crystal Cave. Throughout the cave, weakly acidic groundwater has seeped down through cracks in the marble. This slow flow of water gradually shaped passages by widening the cracks.

Multiple sources of acidic water—whether from several streams or a combination of streams and water seeping through the ground—create a more acidic environment that dissolves the surrounding rock. Rooms often form where two or more sources of water meet. In Crystal Cave, this seems to have happened in the Dome Room and Marble Hall, where water flowing horizontally met water trickling down from above. These rooms lie at the center of the cave's anastomotic mazes. Sixteen passages leave Marble Hall, eleven branch off from the Dome Room and five exit the Phosphorescent Room on the "Wild Tour" route.

Water has not always flowed freely through Crystal Cave. At times, glacial debris washed down from the high country or other geologic activity may have blocked the cave's entrance. Deposits of soil on the cave's shelves, ledges and alcoves mark where gravel and dirt settled out from slow-moving or ponded floodwaters. Most of this material washed away when water again began to flow through the cave, but in protected corners, pockets of soil remain to tell the story of flooding.

As the surrounding water table dropped, water drained from Crystal Cave's passages. As air enters a cave, different processes begin working to create the cave's formations.

Initially, water in surface soils dissolves carbon dioxide, creating weak carbonic acid. The acidic water seeps through cracks in the stone above the cave, dissolving small amounts of marble. As this solution enters cave passages, carbon dioxide escapes into the cave air. The water becomes less acidic and can no longer hold the dissolved stone. Small amounts of rock crystallize on cave surfaces as the mineral *calcite,* a form of calcium carbonate. Calcite and other minerals may also be deposited when water evaporates in a dry or breezy cave passage. Each drop of water deposits a thin coating of minerals. Over thousands of years, layer on layer of these thin deposits grow to become the varied cave formations we see today. Geologists refer to the often-delicate and beautiful growth of these rock structures as *speleothems* or *secondary cave formations.* (See diagrams and photographs on pages 38 and 39.)

Water moves through caves in many ways, dripping, standing in pools, flowing in sheets over rock. Each creates a particular type of cave formation. *Stalactites* hang from ceilings, walls or ledges in three common forms.

• *Soda straws* begin to grow as calcite is deposited in a ring around the outside of a drop of water. As more drops follow, more rings form until a slender, drop-sized tube develops. Sodastraws continue to grow as long as drops flow through this tube to the formation's tip where additional stone is deposited.

• *Curtains, draperies* or *cave bacon* form where water trickles down a cave's wall or ceiling. The water traces a single narrow path, depositing a long, thin calcite curtain in its wake.

• Typical *stalactites,* wide at the base and tapering at a point, often begin as sodastraws. If a hollow sodastraw becomes plugged, water begins to flow over its outside, depositing new rock there. More calcite accumulates at the base of the formation, where the water-acid-stone solution first emerges. Stalactites grow throughout Crystal Cave. The best examples hang near the cave's entrance, in the Curtain, Organ and Dome rooms and in Marble Hall.

Stalagmites form when calcite-carrying water consistently drips onto the same spot on a floor or ledge. The drops splatter as they strike the cave floor, and the splashing water leaves a circular deposit of stone. The small circle may become the outer diameter of the growing stalagmite. The shape and size of the stalagmite depends on the distance the dripping water falls, the number and frequency of the drips, the surface of the cave floor and other factors. In Crystal Cave, look for stalagmites near the cave entrance, in the Junction Room and in Marble Hall.

Sometimes, stalactites grow long enough to reach the cave floor, stalagmites extend up to the ceiling, or a stalactite and stalagmite grow together to form *columns* or *pillars.* Columns can be small or they can be mas-

35

sive, partially filling large rooms. Look for columns in the Dome Room.

Water flowing across a floor, slope or wall produces other formations. Smooth *flowstone* formations often develop on steep or uniform surfaces. You can see flowstone near the cave entrance and in the Organ and Dome rooms.

On rough or slightly sloping surfaces where water pools, calcite builds up around the edges of the pools as *rimstone dams*. As a dam grows it holds back more water, sometimes creating a large pool. Rimstone dams have grown along the cave trail before the Junction Room, in the Junction Room itself and in the Dome Room.

Calcite-rich water dripping into shallow rimstone pools or small pockets on the cave floor may strike small rocks or sand grains and deposit layers of stone around them. The agitation caused by the dripping keeps these new formations, called *cave pearls*, unattached. Often round, smooth and white, cave pearls rarely grow more than an inch in diameter. Pools in the Dome Room contain cave pearls.

Popcorn, cave coral, or *coralloids* form in rimstone pools, or where water has pooled. These small, rough, irregular and often branched deposits resemble their namesakes. Popcorn dots the ceiling of the Junction Room and pools in the Dome Room.

Helectites appear to defy gravity. Seldom associated with cracks, these generally small formations grow directly out of bedrock or soil. Water under pressure, forced through spaces within the rock, leaves behind curling, twisting deposits of calcite. Helectites appear in many forms. Commonly, they branch, divide, twist and turn in no apparent pattern. Some resemble cave popcorn, others, defined by their crystal structure, can be very angular. One variety radiates from a central pincushion-like area. Helectites are uncommon in Crystal Cave and have formed in only a few places.

Shields are rare formations associated with water under pressure and cracks in cave walls, ceilings or floors. They form as two flat, oval plates growing from a crack. Shields often have other formations, such as stalactites or helectites, growing from them. Crystal Cave contains at least fifty shields and similar structures, possibly more than any other cave in California. Most of these lie away from the tour route, but you can see shields on the ceiling of the Organ Room, directly above the Organ formation.

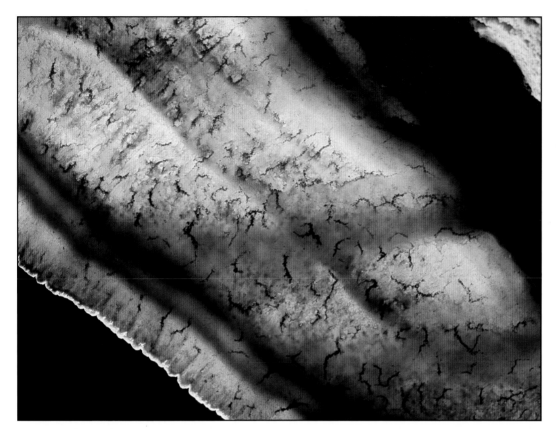

Left:
Close-up view of a cave curtain. Lighting behind the curtain reveals the partially translucent nature of this formation. Dark bands are layers of various mineral impurities deposited as the formation grew. Lighter bands are more pure calcite.

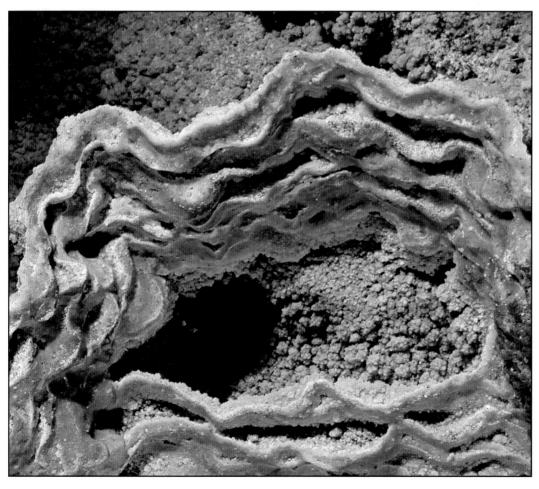

Left:
Crystals in a fossil pool

The shaded illustrations represent the growth of cave formations. Lighter areas were layed down first, while darker areas were deposited later. Calcite cave formations come in a large variety of shapes, many of which are represented here.

Speleothems (as geologists know them) are formed when water on the surface above the cave dissolves small amounts of naturally occurring carbon dioxide gas, creating a weak acid known as carbonic acid. Carbonic acid, seeping through cracks in the cave ceiling, dissolves small amounts of marble. When the mixture of water, carbon dioxide and dissolved rock emerges into the cave environment, generally in the form of drops, carbon dioxide escapes into the cave air. The water-based mixture becomes less acidic and can no longer contain the dissolved marble. The marble is deposited as small crystals of calcite, which build-up through long periods of time to become cave formations.

The different shapes and patterns of cave formations are created by the different ways that the water moves across the many surfaces of a cave passage.

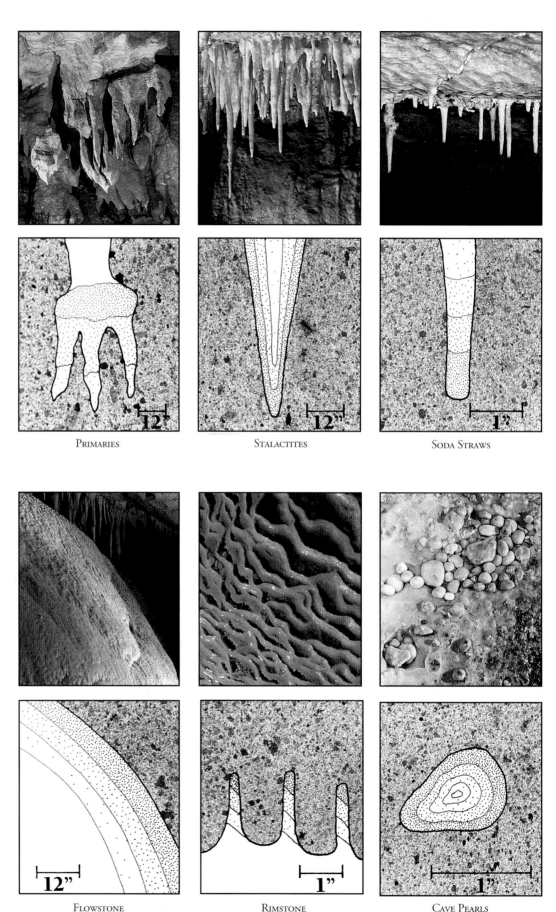

PRIMARIES

STALACTITES

SODA STRAWS

FLOWSTONE

RIMSTONE

CAVE PEARLS

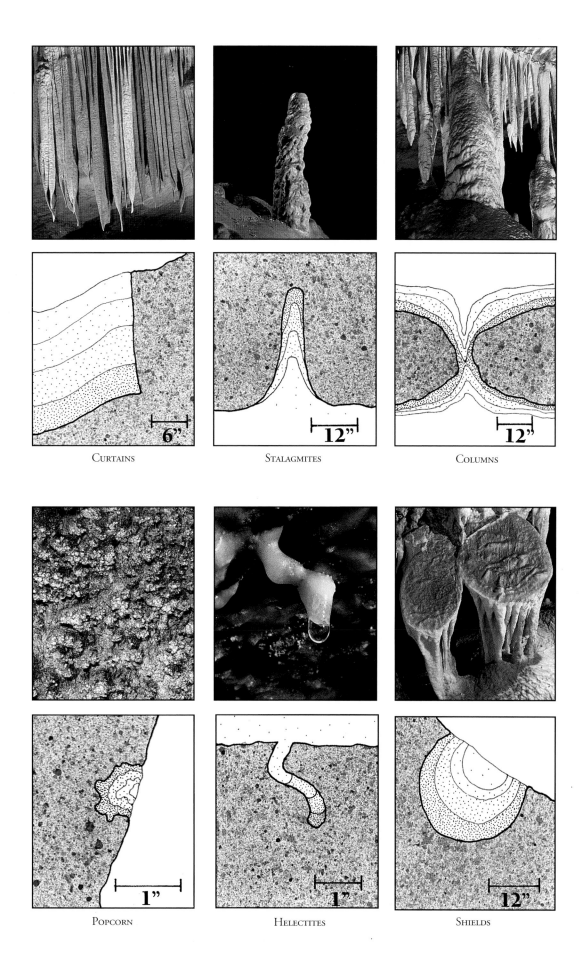

CURTAINS

STALAGMITES

COLUMNS

POPCORN

HELECTITES

SHIELDS

LITTLE BROWN BAT
Myotis lucifugus

BIG BROWN BAT
Eptesicus fugcus

TOWNSEND'S BIG-EARED BAT
Plecotus townsendii

LONG EARED BAT
Myotis evotis

WESTERN PIPISTRELLE
Pipistrellus hesperus

PALLID BAT
Antrozous pallidus

MEXICAN FREE-TAILED BAT
Tadarida brasiliensus

LUMP-NOSED BAT
Plecotus rafinesquii

4

CREATURES OF CRYSTAL CAVE

Without lights, trails and warm clothes, caves would be uncomfortable places for people to visit. But for other animals, caves do provide a home. There they live without sunlight or the changes of temperature and humidity found on the surface. Through countless generations, these species have adapted to the conditions found in caves.

Crystal Cave is home to a number of these specialized creatures. Their specialization allows them to survive here, but also makes them vulnerable to any changes in the cave's environment. Their survival, and the survival of the cave's small, but vital, ecosystem depends on the proper management and protection of Crystal Cave.

Biologists divide cave-dwelling animals into three groups:
• *Troglobites,* animals restricted to caves;
• *Troglophiles,* those who live both in caves and on the surface; and
• *Trogloxenes,* who regularly visit caves but cannot complete their life cycles in subterranean environments.

Troglobites have adapted to live exclusively in caves and could not survive outside them. Often eyeless, they lack pigment and may differ in other ways from their surface-dwelling relatives. Blind white cavefish, cave salamanders and cave crayfish are the most well-known troglobites. They're not found in the western United States, where cave systems tend to be small and isolated. Crystal Cave's troglobites are all small *invertebrates*— animals without backbones.

Park staff first noticed life in the cave stream in 1991 when they found isopods, small crustaceans related to sow bugs or roly-polies. Fully adapted to the cave environment, with no eyes or coloration, they eat organic matter such as leaves and twigs carried into the cave by the stream. Other troglobites in Crystal Cave include a species of white millipede and eyeless centipedes. Biologists believe these species are found only in Crystal Cave.

Troglophiles live and can complete their life cycles in caves, but can also live on the surface in other suitable environments. Crystal Cave's troglophiles include at least ten species of spiders. Commonly seen, especially on the "Wild Cave" tour, is *Nesticus sylvestrii.* These small, light-brown spiders weave webs of dozens of strands spun inside cracks along the cave's walls. Their prey includes other troglophiles such as fungal-gnat flies and small, silver-colored springtails from the order *Collembola,* Crystal Cave's most common inhabitant.

Another interesting spider is a representative of the genus *Pimoa.* These moderately-sized spiders have a shiny black body with large brown spots. They spin large, tangled webs. They live only near the cave's entrance, where some light penetrates. This species lives only here and in several other cave entrances in the Yucca Creek drainage. Ten miles to the north, in Kings Canyon National Park, a related species lives in another group of caves.

Other troglophiles living in Crystal Cave include two species of millipede, one of which can create its own light with glowing body parts. Crickets with very long antennae of the genus *Tropidischia* can sometimes be found in the cave as well.

Cave-dwelling species of bats are the best-known trogloxenes. Bats can be found within Crystal Cave in small groups or as individuals, particularly in the passages of the Catacombs and near the cave entrance at dusk and dawn.

All bat species in Sequoia and Kings Canyon National Parks eat night-flying insects. Bats devour huge numbers of insects to fuel their high metabolism and power their flight. A study of midwestern bats revealed that a single bat ate more than twenty-thousand mosquitos and fifty-thousand moths in one summer. Bats play a vital role in maintaining a balance of animal populations and help keep mosquito populations under control.

Four bats—the little brown bat, *Myotis lucifugus;* the big brown bat, *Eptesicus fuscus;* the California myotis, *Myotis californicus;* and the rare Townsend's big-eared bat, *Plecotus townsendii,* may regularly use Crystal Cave as a daytime roost. Few are present at any one time. The long-eared bat, *Myotis evotis;* the western pipistrelle, *Pipistrellus hesperus;* the pallid bat, *Antrozous pallidus;* the Mexican free-tailed bat, *Tadarida brasiliensis mexicana;* and the lump-nosed bat, *Corynorhinus rafinesquii,* may visit the cave occasionally.

Another trogloxene, the Ensantina, *Ensantina escholtzi*—a black salamander with orange spots—lives in moist areas near the cave's entrances. Rodents, including the brush mouse, *Peromyscus boylii;* the deer mouse, *Peromyscus maniculatus;* and the dusky-footed woodrat, *Neotoma fuscipes,* also live here. They're rarely seen, but seem to be common judging from the many acorns and droppings they leave in the cave.

Large mammals also use the cave. Black bears, *Ursus americanus,* may have hibernated here. Ring-tailed cats, *Bassariscus astutus,* occasionally forage for food near the entrance. Another large mammal uses Crystal Cave for scientific studies, to satisfy curiosity and simply for entertainment. Humans, *Homo sapiens sapiens,* have long been trogloxenes—seeking out caves for shelter, religious purposes, research and adventure.

Right:
Ensantina salamanders can be found in damp areas near Crystal Cave's entrance.

Below:
Ringtail cats regularly wander into the Spider Web Gate Entrance of Crystal Cave during their nightly search for food.

5

THE CAVES OF SEQUOIA AND KINGS CANYON

More than 225 caves riddle the rocks of the southern Sierra. One-hundred-seventy of these lie in the western third of Sequoia and Kings Canyon National Parks. Like Crystal Cave, most developed through the work of acidic groundwater.

Rangers monitor the Parks' caves, and access to them is limited to protect both visitors and the caves. Would-be explorers face deep pits with sudden drop-offs, underground waterfalls, near-freezing temperatures, mazes and other life-threatening hazards. To visit these caves requires a tolerance for darkness, tight spaces and cold along with the stamina and strength for time-consuming ropework. Even then, inexperienced cavers may destroy delicate formations or unintentionally kill cave-dwelling animals just through the disturbances they create passing through caves.

Lilburn Cave is the longest cave in Sequoia and Kings Canyon, and one of the longest in the western United States, with more than fourteen miles of mapped and explored passages. Like those of Crystal Cave, Lilburn's passages wind and interconnect in an anastomotic maze. In Lilburn, five cave streams and sinkholes above the cave allow water to enter the cave from many points. These multiple water sources have carved one of the most complex caves in the United States.

The cave lies in a block of marble three-thousand feet long, seven-hundred feet wide and four-hundred feet deep: twenty-three times larger than the one in which Crystal Cave formed.

Beautiful blue-and-white-banded marble adorns the walls of many passages. Compared to Crystal Cave, Lilburn has few formations, but the formations here are often beautiful. A wide variety of minerals in the rock have colored formations yellow, blue, black, green and other uncommon hues.

Lilburn has been set aside for scientific study. A national organization, the Cave Research Foundation, coordinates expeditions into the cave to map passages and to study the cave's sediments, hydrology, mineralogy and biology.

In July 1988, a group of Bay Area cavers and park employees entered Hurricane Crawl Cave for the first time. Since then, more than a mile-and-a-half of passages have been explored. Many rare and beautiful cave formations, including shields, helectites and calcite and gypsum crystals decorate the cave. Hurricane Crawl also contains several large rooms. The biggest—Pumpkin Palace—has orange flowstone and curtains along its walls and a large white candlelike stalagmite. Cave biologists have discovered several new species of cave-adapted invertebrates in Hurricane Crawl.

Exploration of the cave continues, with researchers regularly finding new passages and rooms. In 1992, they discovered a connection between Hurricane Crawl and another cave nearby—adding to the known length of the cave system. In 1993, they explored the cave's most northerly passage, a low crawlway that appears to flood in the spring.

The nearly pristine features of Hurricane

Three views of the Enchanted River section of Lilburn Cave. The striped walls and red stains are the natural colors of this beautiful polished marble passage. Notice the specialized equipment and clothing used by the cave explorers.

Crawl require careful protection. The National Park Service allows access only to scientists and skilled cave-explorers working on approved projects. Even they may enter the cave only four times per year, and seventeen areas of the cave are closed to all entry.

High-elevation valleys in the southern sections of the Park hold extensive cave systems, including Panorama, Cirque, Jordon and others. Numerous entrances, active streams and waterfalls, near-freezing temperatures and scoured and polished white-and-black marbles characterize caves in these areas. Like Crystal and Lilburn, many feature mazelike passages carved by sinking streams. These caves often flood in spring, so formations rarely develop in them. Exploration in this area continues, but the most extensive discoveries in the high-altitude caves occurred in the 1950s, 1960s and the late 1970s.

Beginning in the 1800s, people discovered Lost Soldier's, Clough, Palmer, Paradise and other low-elevation caves in the southern part of the Park. Ancient patterns of water flow created these caves. Eventually, lowering water tables left them dry. Cave tunnels of this type are called *fossil passages* because they record extinct, or fossil, water-flow patterns.

Some of these caves have been badly damaged by miners, curious souvenir hunters and careless cavers. They removed cave formations, carved and wrote their names on cave walls and tracked mud over expanses of white floors and walls. In spite of the damage, many beautiful, interesting features remain. Park Service management policies now encourage the clean-up and restoration of these caves. Locked entrances guard some and many require entry permits from the National Park Service.

The caves of Sequoia and Kings Canyon National Parks hold experiences and information, illustrate geologic processes and provide habitat for rare and unique animals. Caves enhance the beauty and rich natural history of the area and have their own intrinsic value. Protected and managed wisely, they can be studied, enjoyed and marveled at for generations to come.

How does the length of Crystal Cave compare to other caves?

Note: The mapped length of caves may change rapidly as new passages are discovered and explored.

LONG CAVES OF CALIFORNIA *(as mapped):*

1. Lilburn Cave, Kings Canyon Natl. Park   14.10 miles
2. Bigfoot Cave, Siskiyou County   13.50 miles
3. Crystal Cave, Sequoia Natl. Park   2.42 miles
4. Church Cave, Fresno County   2.12 miles
5. Hurricane Crawl Cave, Sequoia Natl. Park   1.59 miles
  (Discovered in 1988.)
6. California Caverns, Calaveras County   1.47 miles
7. Glory Cave   1.39 miles
8. Apogee Cave, Siskiyou County   1.30 miles
(Extensive exploration in the early 1990s quadrupled the known length of this cave.)
9. Vanished River Cave   1.14 miles
10. Corkscrew Cave, Siskiyou County   1.05 miles
11. Drystream Cave, Siskiyou County   1.05 miles
12. Brokedown Palace Cave, Siskiyou County   1.05 miles

LONG CAVES OF THE UNITED STATES:

1. Mammoth Cave, Kentucky   348 miles
(Mammoth may soon be found to be connected with nearby Fisher Ridge Cave, which would extend its length to well over 400 miles.)
2. Jewel Cave, South Dakota   99 miles
(Explorations in the southeast section of Jewel Cave are adding rapidly to its known size, which is expected to pass 100 miles in the spring of 1994.)
3. Wind Cave, South Dakota   74 miles
4. Lechuguilla Cave, New Mexico   74 miles
(Lechuguilla, one of the most beautiful caves in the world, was discovered in 1986.)
5. Fisher Ridge Cave, Kentucky   65 miles
(Cavers first entered this cave in 1981. Its known size is growing rapidly as explorers make new discoveries.)
6. Friar's Hole, W. Virginia   43 miles
7. Organ Cave, W. Virginia   39.5 miles
8. Carlsbad Caverns, New Mexico   29.4 miles
9. Blue Spring Cave, Tennessee   28.3 miles
10. Crevice Cave, Missouri   28.2 miles
11. Cumberland Caverns, Tennessee   27.6 miles
12. Sloans Valley Cave, Kentucky   24.6 miles
13. Xanadu Cave, Tennessee   24 miles

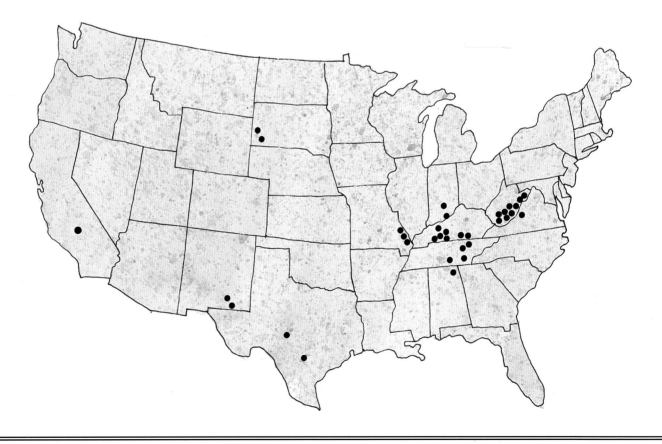

14. The Hole, W. Virginia	23 miles
15. Whigpistle Cave, Kentucky	22.5 miles
16. Culverson Creek Cave, W. Virginia	20.8 miles
17. Binkley's Cave, Indiana	20 miles
18. Blue Springs Cave, Indiana	20 miles
19. Hicks Cave, Kentucky	19.8 miles
20. Honey Creek Cave, Texas	19.1 miles
21. Scott Hollow Cave, W. Virginia	18.2 miles
22. Mountain Eye Cave, Tennessee	18 miles
23. Windymouth Cave, W. Virginia	18 miles
24. Butler-Sinking Creek, Virginia	17.2 miles
25. Thornhill Cave, Kentucky	16.7 miles
26. Moore Cave, Missouri	16.5 miles
27. McClung Cave, W. Virginia	16.4 miles
28. Mystery Cave, Missouri	15.8 miles
29. Fern Cave, Alabama	15.6 miles
30. Cave Creek Cave, Kentucky	15 miles
31. Benedicts Cave, W. Virginia	14.8 miles
32. Powells Cave, Texas	14.2 miles
33. Bone-Norman Cave, W. Virginia	14.1 miles
34. Lilburn Cave, California	**14.1 miles**

LONG CAVES OF THE WORLD:

1. Mammoth Cave, United States	348 miles
2. Optimisticeskaja, Ukraine	114 miles
3. Jewel Cave, United States	99 miles
4. Holloch, Switzerland	97 miles
5. Siebenhengste-hohgant, Switzerland	78.3 miles
6. Wind Cave, United States	74 miles
7. Lechuguilla Cave, United States	71 miles
8. Ozernaja, Ukraine	69 miles
9. Gua Air jernih, Malaysia	63 miles
10. Ojo Guarena, Spain	60.5 miles

GLOSSARY

AMMONITES: A large group of extinct, shelled mollusks which lived in the ocean two-hundred-million years ago.

ANASTOMOSE: To communicate or connect with each other through common canals. In caves, a series of many irregular and repeatedly connected small solution tubes or passages. On the surface, a braided stream.

ARAGONITE: A mineral with the same chemical composition as calcite, $CaCO_3$, but with a different—orthorhombic—crystal system.

BATHOLITH: A single mass of igneous rock.

BRYOZOANS: Colonial marine animals that secrete a calcium-based or horny covering and which occur in a wide variety of forms and structures.

CALCITE: A mineral, calcium carbonate, $CaCO_3$, with hexagonal and rhombohedral crystal systems.

CALCIUM CARBONATE: A solid compound occurring in nature in limestone, cave formations, marble, dolomite and other calcite rocks.

CARBONIC ACID: A naturally occurring acid, H_2CO_3, formed by the combination of water, H_2O, and carbon dioxide, CO_2, involved in the creation of caves.

CAVE PEARLS: Small, generally round calcite cave formations formed by dripping water.

COMPASS: A device that uses the Earth's magnetic field to determine north and other directions.

CLINOMETER: A device that measures the angle (in degrees or percentage) of slopes.

CRINOIDS: Ocean animals related to sea stars and sea urchins, with branched, feathery arms. Some, called sea lilies, have long stalks attached to the bottom.

CRUST: The five- to fifteen-mile thick outer shell of the Earth.

CURTAIN: A calcite formation created by rivulets of water flowing across an overhanging surface. These formations resemble cloth curtains or draperies.

DIORITE: A plutonic igneous rock composed of plagioclase feldspar and small amounts of biotite, pyroxene, or quartz. (see Plutonic)

FORAMINIFERANS: Small, ocean-living protozoans with calcium carbonate skeletons.

GRANITE: A plutonic igneous rock composed of feldspar and quartz, and smaller amounts of muscovite, or biotite. (see Plutonic)

HELECTITE: Generally a small calcite formation found in a variety of unusual shapes. Created by pressurized water.

IGNEOUS: Rocks formed from molten material

ISOPODS: One of many kinds of crustaceans with seven pairs of legs. Some species live on land, others in water.

KARST: An area of the surface of the Earth characterized by springs, sinking streams, sinkholes, caves and other features formed by the action of ground water on carbonate rock such as limestone or marble. A type of topography named for the Karst Region of Eastern Europe.

LIMESTONE: A layered sedimentary rock consisting chiefly of calcium carbonate.

LINE PLOT: In cave surveys, a drawing of the lines created during the survey and representing the cave passages.

MARBLE: A metamorphic rock composed chiefly of calcite

METAMORPHIC ROCK: Rocks whose original texture and structure has been altered by heat and pressure.

NATIONAL SPELEOLOGICAL SOCIETY: A national organization based in Huntsville, Alabama, which formed in 1941 to promote cave conservation, research, management and exploration.

PANGAEA: The super-continent formed at the end of the Mississippian Period composed of all existing continental land masses.

PHREATIC: The zone of saturation. Below the water table.

PLATE: Geologic term for a portion of the Earth's crust. The surface of the Earth is composed of a series of separate plates that slowly move. Their movement creates mountains, volcanic activity, earthquakes and other tectonic features and events.

PLUTONIC: A general term applied to igneous rocks that have formed and crystallized at great depth below the surface of the Earth.

POROSITY: A term used to describe spaces or openings within bedrock. Porosity involving vertical fractures, inter-granular pores, and bedding partings or exfoliation separations are important in cave development.

PRECIPITATE: In chemistry and cave development, to separate and solidify a substance from a solution.

PRIMARY FORMATIONS: Bedrock remnants within a cave that occur in a wide variety of forms including rough pendants that resemble stalactites. Also called speleogens.

RADIOLARIANS: Free-living, one-celled marine protozoans with tiny shells composed of silica.

RECHARGE: In cave geology used to describe the source of water involved in a cave's development. Important types of recharge include a diffuse water source, rising acidic or thermal water, multiple sources of surface water and a single source, often called a sinking stream.

RIMSTONE: A calcite formation that grows around the margin of pooled water.

ROOF PENDANTS: Older rocks projecting down into a batholith of plutonic igneous rock.

SCHIST: A metamorphic rock often composed of marine sediments, identified by its ability to split into flakes or slabs.

SECONDARY CAVE FORMATIONS: Deposits within a cave generally formed after air fills cave passages. Often formed of calcite, but may be composed of other minerals including aragonite and gypsum. Also called speleothems.

SEDIMENTARY ROCK: Rocks formed by the accumulation of sediments on land or in water, usually with a layered structure.

SHIELD: A calcite formation that may develop where pressurized water moves through cracks in bedrock

SHOT: In cave surveys, a set of information that includes distance, direction and inclination along a section of cave passage.

SINKHOLES: Depressions in the Earth's surface in which water collects and is channeled into subterranean pathways or cave passages. A component of karst topography. Sinkholes may vary in size from a few square feet to many square miles.

SODASTRAW: A calcite formation formed from repeated deposits by single drops of saturated water. Sodastraws are a type of stalactite.

SPELEOGEN: Bedrock remnants within a cave that occur in a wide variety of forms including rough pendants that resemble stalactites. Also called primary formations.

SPELEOTHEMS: Deposits within a cave generally formed after air filled the cave passage. Often formed of calcite, but may be composed of other minerals including aragonite and gypsum. Also called secondary cave formations.

SPRINGTAILS: An order of small insects with many species, several of which are important to food chains in caves in Sequoia and Kings Canyon National Parks.

STALACTITE: A calcite formation created by dripping water that grows down from cave ceilings, walls or ledges.

STALAGMITE: A calcite formation that grows up from a cave floor or ledge where water drips down from above.

SUBDUCTION: A process where one plate plunges beneath another where two or more of the Earth's crustal plates collide. Usually oceanic plates sink below continental plates.

SURVEY STATIONS: In cave surveys, the points along a cave passage that lie at the ends of each shot.

TRILOBITES: An extinct diverse group of crustaceans that lived throughout the Paleozoic Era.

TROGLOBITES: Animals that live only in caves and complete their life cycles there.

TROGLOPHILES: Animals that live within caves and on the surface.

TROGLOXENES: Animals that regularly visit caves, but spend most of their lives on the surface and complete their life cycles there.

VADOSE: The zone of aeration, above the level of the water table.

WATER TABLE: The upper limit of the portion of ground where openings within soil or rock are water-filled or saturated. The area below this limit is called the phreatic zone and the area above is known as the vadose zone.